MEMBERS OF ONE ANOTHER

How to Thrive in the Body of Christ

Jeff Archer

2018 One Stone Press.
All rights reserved. No part of this book may be reproduced in any form without written permission of the publisher.

Published by:
One Stone Press
979 Lovers Lane
Bowling Green, KY 42103

Printed in the United States of America

ISBN: 978-1-941422-36-6

Supplemental Materials Available:
➢ Answer Key
➢ Downloadable PDF

www.onestone.com

CONTENTS

1	"Members of one another"	7
2	"Be like-minded toward one another" Part 1	11
3	"Be like-minded toward one another" Part 2	15
4	"Receive one another" Part 1	19
5	"Receive one another" Part 2	23
6	"Bear with one another"	27
7	"Bear one another's burdens"	31
8	"Admonish one another"	35
9	"Encourage one another"	39
10	"Forgive one another"	43
11	"Submit to and serve one another"	47
12	"Love one another" Part 1	51
13	"Love one another" Part 2	55

Introduction

As a local church, we are to function in harmony as the body of Christ. As in any relationship, working together does not come automatically but takes the concentrated effort of each part. We must LEARN to interact with one another according to the principles of God.

As the Psalmist exclaimed, "Behold, how good and how pleasant it is for brethren to dwell together in unity" (Psa. 133:1). It is in this unity that the light of Jesus will be most brilliantly reflected and the work of the Lord most effectively accomplished.

In this series of lessons, we will focus on a phrase that occurs about 99 times in the New Testament - "one another." In the original language, this phrase is actually from one word "allelon" and is used in about 60 contexts in ways which help us understand our responsibilities to each other. This series of lessons focuses on understanding these contexts to reflect this "one another" Christianity.

These lessons are designed to be **growth sessions**, not **gripe sessions**. If anything is accomplished, each of us must begin with application to self before making constructive comments about the actions of others.

Lesson 1

"Members of one another"

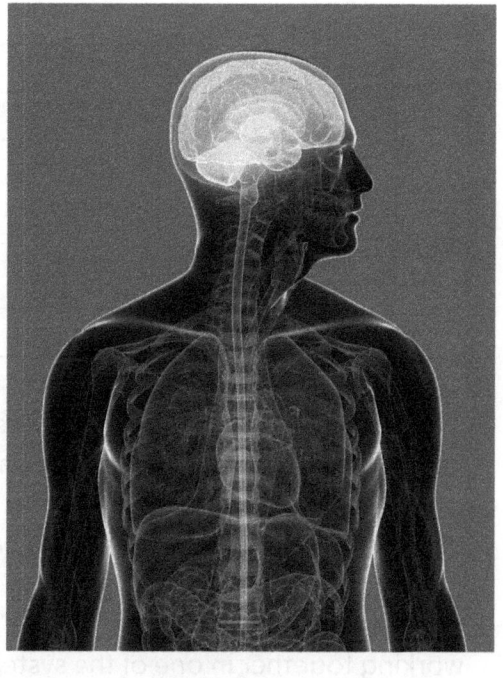

The human body is a wonderful gift from God. It is the most complex physical organism on the planet. There are millions of parts, each with its own identity, functioning together to make one body. Several systems work together seamlessly: the circulatory system, the digestive system, the skeletal system and the nervous system, to name a few. Take, for example, the nervous system. My finger has nerve endings strategically placed just under the skin. When I touch something hot or cold or soothing or painful, those nerves translate the sensation into an electrical impulse which goes through the nerves, through the spinal cord and into the brain which then translates it into something "I" understand, so I respond appropriately. All of this happens in a fraction of a second.

The body of Christ, the church, is a wonderful gift from God. The local church is made up of many different, independent people who possess a variety of talents and strengths in various quantities and combinations. Yet, the purpose of God is for us to function as one.

In this lesson, we would like to explore how we are the **body** of Christ.

The Divine Imperative

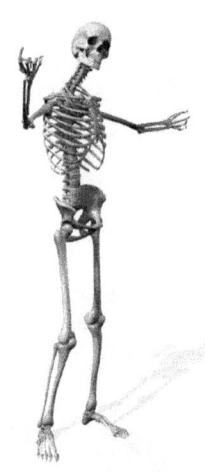

Please read Romans 12:3-8 before answering the following questions.

1. In what sense are we "many" and in what sense are we "one body" (Rom. 12:5)? _____
_____
_____
_____
_____
_____

2. How does "in Christ" define who we are as a body (Rom. 12:5)? _____
_____
_____

3. **Discussion:** Paul said, "all members do not have the same function" in verse 4. In our physical bodies we have many systems with many parts in each system working in harmony to accomplish any task. So, is the body of Christ many systems with many parts working together to accomplish the work of the Lord. The working of each part "causes growth of the body for the edifying of itself in love" (Eph. 4:16). List the number of parts working together in one of the systems of our local church - the teaching program. _____
_____
_____

Which part is unnecessary? _____

4. What is the difference in emphasis between being a member of the church and being a "member of one another" (Rom. 12:5)? _____
_____
_____
_____

5. If I am playing basketball and am poked in the eye, what happens? Does only my eye react? No, my eyelid closes. My hands come to cover my eye. My feet are still, my back bends forward. My brain focuses on my eye to evaluate the damage and properly respond. Debate is not necessary with my hands or my feet to care for the eye. When my eye hurts, I hurt. Discussion: What happens when Satan "pokes" the local body of Christ in "the eye" and why does the body react in this way? _____

_____

_____

6. What "gifts" did Paul list (Rom. 12:6-8)? _____

_____

   A. What other gifts are present within our local body? _____

   _____

7. From where did these gifts come (Rom. 12:6)? _____

   _____

8. What are we to do with the gifts we have been given (Rom. 12:6-8)? ___

   _____

   A. How does a Christian find out which gift(s) he possesses? _____

   _____

   _____

10 Members of One Another

Lesson 2

"Be like-minded toward one another" Part 1

The longest recorded prayer of Jesus on the night before His death is found in John 17. Jesus prayed for Himself, His apostles and us - "those who will believe in Me through their word." What was His desire for us on the night before He endured His own pain and agony on the cross? "...That they all may be one, as You, Father, are in Me and I in You" (John 17:21). God has lived in harmony from all eternity. The unity exemplified by the Father, Son, and Holy Spirit is seamless. In this prayer, Jesus invites us into the unity of God. The expressed will of Jesus for His followers is to be united, in harmony and like-minded with God and each other.

The Divine Imperative

1. What is the basis for our "like-mindedness" (Rom. 15:5)? _____
_____

   A. If we are "like-minded," what will we be able to accomplish as one (Rom. 15:6)? _____

2. If we are to have the same mind, on what will each of our minds NOT be focused (Rom. 12:16)? _____
_____

3. On what does God want each of us to focus our mind? To put it another way, how can we enter into God's unity (Col. 3:1-4)? _____
_____
_____

4. **Discussion:** The church is the "called out" of God from the world. We come to Him with differences in the areas of: race, culture, education level, economic advantage, personality traits, etc. We are not the "same" in many ways. However, God wants each of us to come together and have the "same mind" by focusing on the things of Christ. All of the differences that may divide the world do not divide us because what we have in common in Christ is of greater value to each of us than those things that may divide. What are some of the differences within this local church which we have not allowed to divide us and why? _____

_____

_____

Keep the Unity of the Spirit

5. What is our responsibility according to Ephesians 3:3? _____

_____

   A. When Paul listed the 7 "ones" which surround God, what did he list first (Eph. 4:4-6)? _____

   B. Is unity possible? _____

6. Why is it important to have "peace with one another" (Mark 9:50)? _____

_____

7. **Discussion:** Seeing a sport's team function as one is amazing. When each member flows together in harmony, the team is stronger than the sum of its parts. This team mentality does not come easily or naturally. "Keeping" this harmony is hard work. If you were the coach of this local church, what qualities would you try to develop for this body to function in the harmony of a team? _____

_____

_____

_____

_____

Mutual Submission to the truth

8. As Jesus prayed for His apostles, what important role would the truth play in maintaining unity (John 17:16-17)? _____

   A. What are some of the practical problems with trying to have unity with Buddhists, Hindus, followers of Islam or those who follow the teachings of denominations? _____

9. How did continuing "steadfastly in the apostles' doctrine" help the new saints in Jerusalem to maintain unity (Acts 2:42)? _____

10. What were the apostles to do to make disciples of Christ (Matt. 28:18-20)? _____

    A. What made these disciples unique: social class, political party, economic status, or something else? _____

    B. How would this help to maintain unity? _____

11. What did Paul want to hear about the church in Philippi (Phil.1:27)? __

14 Members of One Another

Lesson 3

"Be like-minded toward one another" Part 2

Paul's first letter to the Corinthians illustrates some of the practical challenges a local church faces in maintaining unity. The church in Corinth is a case study in what *not* to do. Fortunately, God's solutions to their problems are presented in this letter. These solutions are valid for any local church of any culture and at any time including ours.

Two principles are essential for our like-mindedness. First, as we studied at the end of lesson 2, we must each bow in submission to the truth of Jesus Christ. We will continue to explore that principle in this lesson. Second, we must grant each other liberty in the areas of liberty. This principle will be discussed in lessons 4 and 5.

The Divine Imperative

1. On what basis did Paul command the church at Corinth to "speak the same thing ... be perfectly joined together in the same mind and in the same judgment" (1 Cor. 1:10)? _____
   _____
   _____

   A. For all Christians to speak the "same thing", what "thing" must we speak, what "mind" must we have, what "judgment" must we share?
   _____
   _____

16 Members of One Another

2. Apparently, members of the church in Corinth had an allegiance to Christ PLUS a local preacher/teacher. (1 Cor. 1:11-12; see also 4:6).

   A. What blame does the teacher bear when this happens, what might he do to contribute to it and what can he do to stop it? _____
   _____
   _____

   B. What blame does the student bear when this happens, what might he do to contribute to it and what can he do to stop it? _____
   _____
   _____

3. What is the point of the rhetorical questions of Paul in 1 Corinthians 1:13?
   _____
   _____

The Same Message - "Christ and Him crucified"

4. What is the message that is the basis for our unity (1 Cor. 1:18-24)? ___
   _____

   A. What reaction does each group have to this message?
      1. Jews - _____
      2. Greeks - _____
      3. The saved (both Jew and Greek) - _____
      _____

5. When Paul went to Corinth initially, what did he preach and why (1 Cor. 2:1-5)? _____
   _____

6. What is the source of this message (1 Cor. 2:10)? _____

7. Why did the brethren in Corinth struggle with disunity (1 Cor. 3:1-4)? ___
   _____

8. What is the foundation of the church (1 Cor. 3:11)? _____
   _____

9. What lesson did Paul want each member of the church in Corinth to learn (1 Cor. 4:6)? _____
   Discussion: Based on the principles we have learned from 1 Corinthians 1-4, what are some things that must be done in this local church if it is to be unified? _____
   _____
   _____

Practical Application

10. To speak the same things and be of the same mind and judgment is not just a general commitment to follow the teachings of Christ. Christ's will is expressed in how we are to function as a group in many specific areas. In what areas did the church of Corinth need to "speak the same thing"? Please note that preaching "Christ and Him crucified" is a message that contains more than the basic facts of Jesus' crucifixion.
    1 Cor. 5 - _____
    1 Cor. 6 - _____
    1 Cor. 7 - _____

11. **Discussion:** Have there been issues that have arisen in the history of this local church where unity, based on the "message of the cross," was maintained? Do you see issues on the horizon that may challenge the unity of this group? What can you do to promote unity? _____
    _____
    _____

Lesson 4

"Receive one another" Part 1

Note the difference in the following situations.

Situation 1 - A man wrote the church an e-mail, "Hey! I am John and looking for a "gay-friendly" church where my boyfriend, Chip, and I may worship. Are you a 'gay-friendly' church?" I wrote back, "John, If being a 'gay-friendly' church means that we will share the gospel with you and help you overcome sinful practices, then the answer is 'yes.' Since you have defined yourself as homosexual, that would be one of the first things we can discuss. God offers forgiveness for you in Jesus Christ just like He did the Corinthians (1 Cor. 6:9-11). If being 'gay-friendly' means we will turn a blind eye to a direct violation of the will of God, then the answer is 'no.' What kind of church would we be if we do not follow plain Biblical teaching? Surely not one that is of Christ." Apparently, we were not speaking "the same thing" because John did not come.

Situation 2 - A young man started visiting our services. He was obviously from a different background. He had tattoos, wore baggy clothes and a baseball cap to services. One of the members asked me, "Is anyone going to say something to him about that hat?" I said, "I guess that hat bothers you? Do you see it as a matter of doctrine or culture?" He said, a bit flustered, "I don't know, I just don't like it."

As we work on being unified, we will be faced with the question, "Is this belief a part of the doctrine of Christ or my own opinion about the doctrine of Christ?" The answer to that question is significant. The Lord demands mutual submission to the truth in areas where He has spoken (lessons 2 and

3) and mutual acceptance in our differences in areas where He has granted liberty (lessons 4 and 5). In areas where God has stated His truth, Christians are united in following what He says. In areas where God has given us the liberty to hold our judgments, Christians are united in accepting each other in our differences.

The Divine Imperative

1. With what command did Paul begin and end his teaching in Romans 14:1 through 15:7? _____
   _____

2. What words did Paul use to characterize differences between brethren (Rom. 14:1; 15:1)? _____
   _____

3. Note the contrast in the "weak" (Rom. 14:1) and the "strong" (Rom. 15:1). Weak and strong in reference to what? _____
   _____

4. What was an area of dispute among the Romans (Rom. 14:2, 14)? _____
   _____

Oftentimes the *pagans* sacrificed animals to their false gods. A portion of the sacrifice was burned as a sacrifice, a portion was given to the priest for his services and a portion was taken home to eat. The pagan would have eaten this meat as an act of worship to his false god and therefore sinned.

For the *Jews*, the distinction between clean and unclean meat was a part of the observance of the Mosaic Law and would have governed their daily diet from birth. In Christianity, that distinction is erased.

Becoming a Christian presented a particular problem for the pagan and the Jew, especially for the "weak." Even though God permitted the eating of any meat, the weak could not separate the sinful eating from the permitted eating.

5. What was another area of dispute among the Romans (Rom. 14:5)? ____
_____
_____

The *pagans* participated in many festivals associated with false gods. Participating in these festivals was sinful since they contained elements directly connected with the worship of false gods. They also contained other elements of community and family which were not sinful in and of themselves.

The *Jews* participated in various feasts commanded in the Mosaic Law. These feasts had elements of direct significance with the covenant made on Sinai and other elements connected with community and family.

Becoming a Christian presented a dilemma to the pagan and to the Jew, especially for the "weak." Can one participate in a festival without partaking in sin?

Basis for Acceptance

6. On what basis are we to receive one another?
    A. Rom. 14:3 - _____
    B. Rom. 14:4 - _____
    C. Rom. 14:8 - _____
    D. Rom. 14:10 - _____
    E. Rom. 15:7 - _____

What are we to do?

7. What should not be the attitude of those on each side of the issue (Rom. 14:3, 10)? _____
_____

8. What is each individual Christian's responsibility toward his own convictions (Rom. 14:5, 22-23)? _____
_____
_____

9. What should be our attitude (Rom. 14:13)? _____

_____

Note: Being careful not to put a "stumbling block" in front of our brother or "offending" a brother does NOT mean that we can't do something that "bothers or upsets" him. Paul is talking to the strong in the faith not to cause a brother to "stumble" or "sin." Paul is concerned about a weak brother being emboldened to do something he believes is wrong because of the example of a strong brother (who may be exercising his right to do something God has given him the liberty to do). When the weak brother violates his conscience, the strong brother shares in his guilt.

10. How can we pursue peace in dealing with these issues (Rom. 14:19)?

_____

_____

11. How could the work of God be destroyed over these issues (Rom. 14:20)?

_____

_____

"Receive one another" Part 2

Lesson 5

There are two extremes: one extreme says that everything regarding our beliefs and practice is black and white and we must agree on everything, the other extreme says that everything is a matter of judgment, so we can differ on everything. The fact is, some things are spelled out in black and white by God, and we must all mutually submit to His will to be unified. Where God has not spelled it out in black and white, He has given us the liberty to make our judgments and be unified by recognizing that liberty to one another also. Determining the difference can be very difficult but is essential.

Principles from Romans 14

1. Receive one another.
2. Strong - Don't despise the weak.
3. Weak - Don't judge the strong.
4. All - Be fully convinced yourself.
5. Don't be a stumbling block.

In this lesson, we continue to examine areas of "scruples" by discussing specific areas of application to the Romans as well as to Christians today.

Practical Application to the Brethren in Rome

Restrictions concerning eating meat:

It is one thing to understand the teaching of the Bible when converted to Christ. It is another thing to incorporate that teaching into entrenched habits associated with error. We must stop sinful practices, but it may also be a struggle to allow ourselves the liberty to practice things that are right in and of themselves which were previously connected with sin.

1. What additional restrictions might the "weak" place on the eating of meats (Rom. 14:2-3)? _____
   _____

2. What is God's teaching concerning eating meats offered to idols (1 Cor. 8:4-6)? _____
   _____

   A. Could all Christians practice this truth (1 Cor. 8:7)? _____
   _____

3. What is God's teaching about eating meats (1 Tim. 4:3-5)? _____
   _____

4. How did Christians practice these truths (Rom. 14:6, 14)? _____
   _____

Observing days:

5. What additional restriction might the pagan or the Jew place on the observance of special days (Rom. 14:5)? _____
   _____
   _____

6. What is God's teaching concerning observing Jewish feast days (Gal. 5:4; Col. 2:16-17)? _____
   _____

7. What is God's teaching concerning having fellowship with pagan worship festivals (2 Cor. 6:14-16; 1 Cor. 10:18-22)? _____
   _____
   _____

8. How did Christians practice these truths (Rom. 14:6)? _____
   _____

Modern Examples

9. Someone is converted from a denomination which teaches that a woman must have long hair and cannot wear any makeup.

   A. What is God's teaching (1 Tim. 2:9; 1 Cor. 11:14-15)? _____
   _____

   B. What might be the potential problems between brethren? _____
   _____

10. Someone is converted from a denomination which teaches that Jesus was born on December 25 and celebrates Christmas as a religious holiday.

    A. What is God's teaching (Luke 2:1-7; 2 Cor. 6:14)? _____
    _____

    B. What might be the potential problems between brethren? _____
    _____
    _____

11. One man refuses to have a TV in his home because of the sexual immorality that is contained in much of the programming. Another man can have a TV but is careful about the programs he chooses to watch.

    A. What is God's teaching (Matt. 5:28)? _____
    _____

    B. What might be the potential problems between brethren? _____
    _____
    _____

12. Give other examples with which you have wrestled. _____
   _____
   _____

   A. What is God's teaching? _____
      _____

   B. What might be the potential problems between brethren? _____
      _____
      _____

Lesson 6

"Bear with one another in love"

The Divine Imperative

1. As members of the body of Christ, we are to be "endeavoring to keep the unity of the Spirit in the bond of peace" (Eph. 4:3). For this unity to be maintained, several attitudes are needed which are listed in Ephesians 4:1-2. The last one listed by Paul is, "bearing with one another in love" (Eph. 4:2). What does "bearing with/forbearance/make allowances for" mean? _____
   _____
   _____

   A. We are not to be bear with our brethren as they continue in sin. In what areas should we bear with one another? _____
      _____
      _____

   B. Why is "love" necessary to fulfill this responsibility? _____
      _____
      _____

2. This same phrase appears in Colossians 3:12-14. What corresponding attitudes surround this phrase and how do they contribute to "bearing with one another in love"? _____
   _____
   _____

   A. List the opposite of each of these attitudes. _____
      _____

3. The church is not made up of the most "socially connected." Who made up the church of Corinth (1 Cor. 1:26)? _____
   _____

4. If we are not bound together by our educational, economic, or social status, what/Who binds us (1 Cor. 1:22-24)? _____
   _____
   _____

Potential Areas of Irritation

In the first century, as in our time, Christians had to bear with one another for a variety of reasons. Since these potential areas of irritation have nothing to do with our salvation, they don't disappear when becoming a Christian. Our mutual relationship with Christ that binds us together must be stronger than any irritant. The areas discussed below often cause division within the world, but they will not within the body of Christ if we "bear with one another in love."

5. *Rich and Poor* - What quality are we NOT to display (James 2:1)? _____
   _____

   A. With what specific problem did James deal (James 2:2-4)? _____
      _____

   B. What might cause tension between brethren of differing economic levels? _____
      _____

   C. To avoid tension and division in this area, what are some practical things we can do to "bear with one another in love"? _____
      _____

6. *Jew and Gentile* - Why was there tension between Jew and Gentile (Gal. 2:11-13)? _____
   _____

A. What might cause tension between brethren of differing cultural or racial backgrounds? _____

_____

B. To avoid tension and division in this area, what are some practical things we can do to "bear with one another in love"? _____

_____

7. *Young and Old* - What potential area of strain was Timothy to avoid (1 Tim. 4:12; 5:1-2)? _____

_____

A. What might cause tension between brethren of differing ages? ____

_____

_____

B. To avoid tension and division in this area, what are some practical things we can do to "bear with one another in love"? _____

_____

8. List other areas of potential irritation. For example, extroverts and introverts, educated and uneducated, etc. _____

_____

A. To avoid tension and division in these areas, what are some practical things we can do to "bear with one another in love"? _____

_____

Lesson 7

"Bear one another's burdens"

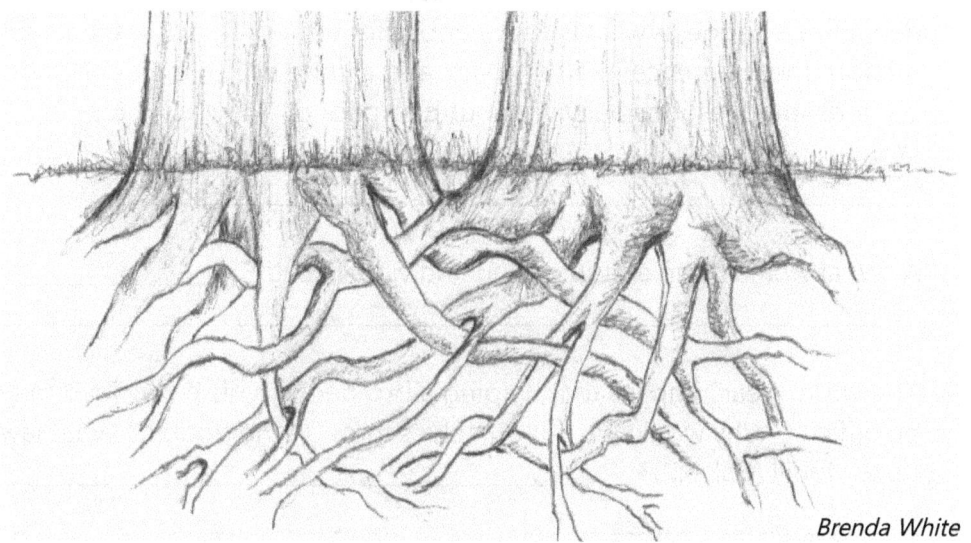

Brenda White

The huge Redwoods of California are amazing. They grow to an average size of 275 feet tall with a diameter of 8 to 12 feet. The oldest Sequoia (in the Redwood family) is 3,500 years old. How can trees so large last so long surviving fires, earthquakes, droughts and pollution?

Part of the answer involves the insulating properties of the bark which is up to 12 inches thick. Another reason is their root system. Rather than each tree reaching deeply into the ground for independent strength, each tree's relatively shallow root base interlocks with those of surrounding trees providing greater mutual strength.

Each Christian can survive the devastating trials of life because of the combined strength of interlocking his roots with those of his brethren.

The Divine Imperative

1. What exhortation does Paul give us in Galatians 6:2? _____
   _____

2. Notice the contrast in "burdens" (Gal. 6:2) and "load" (Gal. 6:5). W.E. Vines says that the difference between "load" and "burden" is, that "load" is simply something to be borne, without reference to its weight, but "burden" always suggests what is heavy or burdensome (page 157). We might think of the difference in a backpack and a crate with handles. What is our individual responsibility with our backpack or "load" (Gal. 6:3-5)? __
   _____
   _____

   A. What would be an example of our individual "load"? _____
      _____

3. The word "bear" implies that helping a brother with his heavy load may be difficult. Why would we put ourselves through the trouble? What law do we fulfill (Gal. 6:2)? _____
   _____

   A. How has Jesus forever changed our definition of love (John 13:34-35)?
      _____

   B. Why should we be willing to help each other in time of need (Gal. 5:13-15)? _____

4. Paul made specific application of the principle of "bear one another's burdens" in Galatians 6:1. What is the connection between the person who has been "overtaken in any trespass" and his need to have help bearing his burden? _____
   _____

   A. Who is specifically asked to help this sinful brother? Why him? ____
      _____

B. What attitudes should the spiritual brother demonstrate as he helps his erring brother? _____

_____

C. What is the goal of this help? _____

_____

Discussion: What might be some particularly dangerous situations when a brother might be "overtaken" in a trespass? _____

_____

_____

5. Does God want us to be concerned about the brother who is caught up in sin (Luke 15:3-7)? _____

_____

6. How far should our love for our brother extend (1 John 3:16-19)? _____

_____

Discussion: What are some practical suggestions to help us when trying to "bear one another's burdens"? For example:

A. Get to know our brethren well enough to know when they are struggling.
B. Keep in confidence when a brother shares his struggles.
C. _____
D. _____
E. _____

Discussion: Tell of a time when someone helped you bear a burden. ____

_____

_____

34 Members of One Another

Lesson 8

"Admonish one another"

We are living in an increasingly impersonal culture where people are more comfortable talking to their smartphones than each other. This culture makes warning a brother of a potential danger difficult. Add to the mix the "don't judge me" posture of the politically correct and then admonishing one another becomes even more challenging. While we do not seek to micro-manage everyone else's life, we are commanded to reach through our discomfort to warn a brother before he makes a mistake that could cost him his soul.

The Divine Imperative

1. What was Paul confident that the brethren in Rome were "able" to do (Rom. 15:14)? _____
   _____

   A. What makes it so hard to admonish a brother? _____
   _____

   B. What are reasons we should admonish a brother in spite of the difficulties? _____
   _____

2. What two qualities made them "able to admonish one another" (Rom. 15:14)? Please explain why each quality is necessary.

   A. _____
   _____

36 Members of One Another

    B. _____

3. Why are the hypocrite's warnings less effective (Matt. 7:3-5)? _____

_____

4. List four things Paul exhorts us to do (1 Thess. 5:14).

    A. _____
    B. _____
    C. _____
    D. _____

5. A few months after writing the first letter to the Thessalonians, Paul wrote a second. In it, he described the action to be taken toward those who "walk disorderly." Please note that this is the same expression used in 1 Thessalonians 5:14 when Paul said to warn the "unruly" (disorderly). What does it mean to "**walk** disorderly" (2 Thess. 3:6)? _____

_____

_____

    A. What specific application did Paul make of the general principle (2 Thess. 3:7-12)? _____

_____

6. In the first letter, Paul said to "warn" those who are unruly. In the second letter, what action is to be taken toward those who "walk" unruly (2 Thess. 3:6)? _____

_____

    A. By what authority did Paul tell us to take this action (2 Thess. 3:6)?

_____

    B. Does this mean that we are never to speak to this brother again (2 Thess. 3:17)? _____

    C. What is the purpose of this action (2 Thess. 3:14)? _____

_____

7. **Discussion:** A brother's involvement in sin is a process. First, he may be tending toward sin, then falling into sin, then walking in sin. Our response also involves a process from warning to withdrawing.

   A. How can we identify how involved with sin a brother might be? ___

   B. How much time should be given between warning a brother and withdrawing from a brother? ___

   C. What are the benefits of carrying out discipline as God instructs? ___

38 Members of One Another

Lesson 9

"Encourage one another"

We have all had people who have believed in us and given words of encouragement which pushed us in a positive direction. Some seem to excel in this talent. We read of a disciple named Joseph in Acts 4:36 who was this type of person. The apostles gave him the nickname of "Barnabas." It means "son of encouragement." What a joy it must have been to have been associated with him! While Joseph/Barnabas excelled in this quality, we are all instructed to develop our ability to encourage one another.

While "admonish one another" emphasizes the negative - warning of the dangers of sin, "encourage one another" emphasizes the positive - exhorting to continue in what is right. Both are part of the balanced relationship we have with our brethren.

The Divine Imperative
(Encouragement with a goal)

1. What did Paul want the brethren in Thessalonica to do (1 Thess. 4:18; 5:11)? _____

2. The term "comfort" or "encourage" comes from a word that means, "literally to call to one's side, to admonish, exhort, to urge one to pursue some course of conduct," (W.E. Vine, p. 600). To "bear one another's burdens" (lesson 7) puts a focus on helping a brother through a difficulty.

"Admonish one another" (lesson 8) puts the focus on helping a brother avoid sin. Where is the focus in "encourage each other"? _____

   A. What is the connection between "encourage" and "edify" (1 Thess. 5:11)? _____

3. Was this an activity these brethren had never practiced in their past (1 Thess. 1:3-4; 3:12-13; 4:9-10; 5:11)? (If not, why did they need to be encouraged to do more?) _____

4. How does the illustration of "as a father does his own children" help define how Paul encouraged his brethren and how we can as well (1 Thess. 2:11) _____

5. Who is responsible for encouraging their brethren?

   A. 2 Tim. 4:2 - _____

   B. Titus 1:9 - _____

   C. Rom. 12:6-8 - _____

   D. Heb. 3:12-13 - _____

Ways to Encourage

6. *Using the power of the truth -*

   A. How did Peter motivate sinners to come to Christ (Acts 2:40)? _____

"Encourage One Another" 41

   B. What truths did Paul tell the Thessalonians about their brethren who had died in the Lord and how did that encourage them (1 Thess. 4:13-18)? _____
   _____

   C. What is the difference in encouraging someone with the truth or with flattery (1 Thess. 2:5)? _____
   _____

   D. Discussion: List an occasion when you have been encouraged by a Christian telling you the truth. _____
   _____

7. *Seeing one another's faith -*

   A. Why did Paul anticipate being encouraged when he visited the brethren in Rome (Rom. 1:11-12)? _____
   _____

   B. **Discussion:** Discuss an occasion when you have been encouraged by seeing a Christian's faith. What was it about seeing a brother's faith that encouraged you? _____
   _____
   _____

8. *Worshipping together -*

   A. When we come together to worship, our main purpose is to praise and glorify God. What other purpose is emphasized by the Hebrew writer (Heb. 10:24-25)? _____
   _____

   B. **Discussion:** Discuss an occasion when you have been encouraged by worshipping with fellow saints. What was it about the mutual worship experience that was encouraging? _____
   _____

The story is told of a member of a church who had been attending services regularly but stopped going. After a few weeks, the preacher went to visit him. It was a chilly evening. The preacher found the man at home alone, sitting before a blazing fire. Guessing the reason for his preacher's visit, the man welcomed him in and led him to a big chair near the fireplace and waited.

The preacher made himself comfortable but said nothing. After some minutes, the preacher took the fire tongs and carefully picked up a brightly burning ember and placed it to the side of the hearth all alone. He then sat back in his chair, still silent. The lone ember's glow diminished slowly. Soon it was cold. Not a word had been spoken since the initial greeting. As the preacher prepared to leave, he picked up the cold, dead ember and placed it back in the middle of the fire. Immediately it began to glow once more with the light and warmth of the burning coals around it. As the preacher reached the door to leave, his host said, "Thank you so much for your visit and especially for the fiery sermon. I will be back in to worship with the saints the next time we meet."

The "manifold wisdom of God" is seen in the church in a variety of ways. One way is that each of us finds greater strength in combining our strength with others. We need one another's encouragement.

Lesson 10

"Forgive one another"

To forgive or not? On one side is a life filled with anger, hatred, and bitterness (all works of the flesh). On the other side is a life filled with love, joy, and peace (all fruit of the Spirit). What stands in-between is the conscious decision to forgive. Forgiveness is a blessing not only for the one forgiven but also for the one who grants forgiveness.

The Divine Imperative

1. Who are we commanded to forgive (Eph. 4:32; Col. 3:13)? _____
   _____

2. Why are "be kind to one another" and being "tenderhearted" essential to forgiveness (Eph. 4:32)? _____
   _____

3. In both of these references, who is used as an example of the way we are to forgive one another? _____
   _____

4. How is God's forgiveness described in Psa. 103:3, 10-12? _____
   _____
   (Please read these verses again replacing the "you" with "me".)

5. **Discussion:** Put into practical terms what it means to be forgiven by a brother. _____
   _____

6. **Discussion:** Put into practical terms what it means to forgive a brother. (Make sure that your answer to question 5 is the same. See Matt. 7:12.) ___

___

7. How much did it cost God to forgive us (Rom. 5:6-8)? ___

___

8. **Discussion:** What are some of the costs of the forgiver when forgiveness is granted? ___

___

   A. Case study: A brother sins against you by spreading an untrue rumor about you. He apologizes and does what he can to correct his error by telling all he can that his rumor was a lie. What might be the cost of forgiveness to you? ___

   ___

   ___

   B. Case study: A brother sins against you by embezzling money from you. He apologizes and promises to do what he can to pay you back in time. What might be the cost of forgiveness to you? ___

   ___

   C. What other examples have you seen where forgiveness demands the sacrifice of the forgiver? ___

   ___

9. What is the responsibility of the one who sins against his brother (Matt. 5:23-24)? ___

___

10. What is the responsibility of the one who is sinned against (Matt. 18:15-17)? _____
_____

11. How often must we forgive (Matt. 18:21-22)? _____

12. Why and how are we to forgive (Matt. 18:23-35)? _____
_____

Lesson 11

"Submit to and serve one another"

On Wednesday, April 27, 2011, an F-5 tornado tore through North Alabama leaving destruction in its wake. My son, Todd was in his house hugging his toilet when the tornado destroyed his home. That Saturday, when roads were barely passable, men from the church where Todd is a member rallied to help. They came equipped with chainsaws, leather gloves and a lot of love. No one had to bark out commands because each submitted to one another as they served their brother. A bond was deepened that day which will last for eternity.

The Divine Imperative

1. To whom are we to submit (Eph. 5:21)? _____

    A. "Submit" means "Primarily a military term, to rank under (lit. to arrange under) to subject oneself to, to obey, be subject to", (W.E. Vine, p. 86). Submit is a voluntary act of humility. It could be translated "obey," but "submit" emphasizes the attitude rather than the action.

    B. How does "in the fear of God" help define our submission? _____

    _____

2. In Gal. 5:13-15, Paul instructed us in how we are to use our liberty in Christ.

   A. If someone did not heed the admonishment of Paul and used his liberty "as an opportunity for the flesh," how might it be manifested in his life (Gal. 5:13)? Also read 1 Cor. 3:2-3; James 3:15-16. _____
   _____
   _____

   B. How *does* Paul want us to use our liberty? _____
   _____

Examples

3. What did Paul do for his brethren and why (Phil. 2:17)? _____
   _____

4. What was Paul confident that Timothy would do for his brethren and why (Phil. 2:19-22)? _____
   _____

5. What did Epaphroditus do for his brethren and why (Phil. 2:25-30)? _____
   _____

6. What did Jesus do for us and why (Phil. 2:5-8)? _____
   _____

Specific Areas of Application

7. *One with another:* What are some specific practical ways brethren at this congregation serve and submit to one another? _____
   _____

8. *Members to elders:* What is the responsibility of members to elders (Heb. 13:17)? _____
   _____

A. What are some specific practical ways that members of this congregation have submitted themselves to the leadership of the elders? _____
_____
_____

9. *Younger to older:* What is the responsibility of the younger to the older (1 Pet. 5:5)? _____
_____

   A. Why should "all of you be submissive to one another" (1 Pet. 5:5)? __
   _____
   _____

   B. What are some specific practical ways that younger members of this congregation have submitted themselves to older members? _____
   _____
   _____

Philosophies of Man

"Greece said, 'Be wise, know yourself!'
Rome said, 'Be strong, discipline yourself!'
Epicureanism says, 'Be sensuous, enjoy yourself!'
Education says, 'Be resourceful, expand yourself!'
Psychology says, 'Be confident, assert yourself!'
Materialism says, 'Be satisfied, please yourself!'
Pride says, 'Be superior, promote yourself!'
Humanism says, 'Be capable, believe in yourself!'

Yourself, yourself, yourself. We're up to here with self? Do something either for yourself or with yourself or to yourself. How very different from Jesus' model and message! No 'philosophy' to turn our eyes inward, He offers rather a fresh and much-needed invitation to our 'me-first' generation. There is a better way. Jesus says, 'Be a servant, give to others!'"

Swindoll, Charles R. (1981). *Improving Your Serve* (pp. 38-39). Waco, TX: Word.

"Love one another" Part 1

Have you ever wondered why geese fly in a "V" formation? As each bird flaps its wings, it creates uplift for the bird immediately following. By flying in "V" formation, the whole flock adds at least 71% greater flying range than if each bird flew on its own. If a goose falls out of formation, it suddenly feels the drag and resistance of trying to go it alone and quickly gets back into formation to take advantage of the lifting power of the bird in front. When the head goose gets tired, it rotates back in the wing, and another goose flies point.

God has placed the instinct within the geese to fly as a team. We, as humans and members of the body of Christ, have to LEARN to fly together. As the goose instinctively puts the benefit of the flock above his interest even being willing to take his turn at the point of the "V," so the Christian chooses in love to put the interest of his brethren above his interest. This mutual love strengthens each one to fly to heights beyond the capability of any one alone.

The Divine Imperative

1. What does God command us to do (1 John 4:7)? _____

_____

2. What is listed first in the "fruit of the Spirit" (Gal. 5:22-23)? _____

3. What was the first thing Paul prayed for on behalf of the church in Philippi (Phil. 1:9)? _____
_____

4. What priority did Peter put on having "love for one another" (1 Pet. 4:8)?
_____
_____

5. What was first in the Hebrew writer's rapid-fire list of exhortations in Hebrews 13? _____
_____

6. How important is our love for one another (1 John 4:8)? _____
_____

7. In what did Paul want the Thessalonian brethren to "abound" (1 Thess. 1:4:9-10)? _____
_____

   A. How did they respond to this challenge (2 Thess. 1:3)? _____
   _____

8. With what are we to "greet one another" (I Pet. 5:14; Rom. 16:16; 1 Cor. 16:20)? _____
_____

Love Defined

9. What is the definition of "love" (agape)? _____
_____

10. Put "God is love" in your own words (1 John 4:7-8). _____
_____

11. How was the love of God "manifested" (1 John 4:9)? _____
_____

"Love One Another" Part 1 53

    A. What does this expression teach us about our love for one another?
    _____

12. Did we love God first or did He love us first (1 John 4:10, 19)? _____
_____

    A. What does this teach us about our love for one another? _____
_____
_____

13. Jesus has given us a "new" command in John 13:34. (Note: The Greeks used two words that meant "new." One referred to something that had never been seen before. Jesus did not use this word. The word used here for "new" meant, "new and improved." Jesus redefined and improved on the commandment to love by loving us in a revolutionary way.) Explain Jesus' redefinition of love? _____
_____

    A. What does this teach us about our love for one another? _____
_____

Lesson 13

"Love one another" Part 2

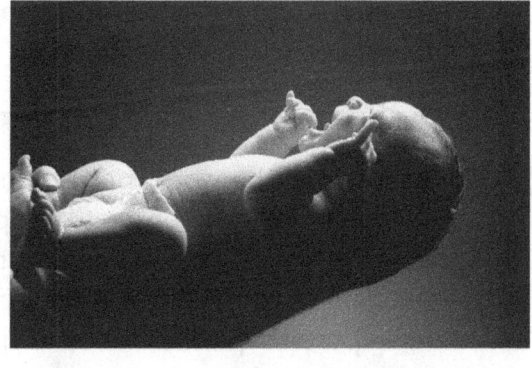

After the end of the cold war, doctors from the US went to witness the birth process in the former Soviet Union. In the typical Russian procedure, the mother was put into the hospital for a week to 10 days. During this time the husband wasn't allowed to see his wife or newborn child except for brief daily visits. During the birth process, the mother was heavily sedated so that she remembered little or nothing of the birth and the baby wasn't brought to her until two or three days after the birth.

The US doctors were then given the opportunity to demonstrate their procedure. They did not heavily sedate the woman; the father was present, and the baby was placed in the mother's arms within moments of birth. The joy of the mother as she held her new baby brought tears to the eyes of the Russian doctors. They had never seen the immediate bonding that took place. This bond of love between father and mother and their newborn child is precious and God-given. God wants more than a man, woman, and their children simply sharing the same living quarters. He wants them to be bound together as a family by love.

As the church of the Lord, we are the spiritual family of God. Our bond of love is precious and God-given as well.

Bond of Perfection

1. In Colossians 3, Paul listed a number of attitudes and actions we are to "put off" and others we are to "put on." What are we to put on "above all these things" (Col. 3:14)? _____
   _____
   _____

   A. The word "bond" was used to refer to a sash or a belt that held clothing together. It was also used of ligaments which hold the body together. In what sense is love our "bond"? _____
      _____

   B. **Discussion:** The word "perfection" does not mean flawlessness or sinlessness. When referring to people it means "a state of maturity or being full-grown." When referring to things it means "being brought to a state of completion or being finished." Paul had just listed several important qualities for us to "put on" in Col. 3:12-13. How does love bind all of these qualities together bringing them to a state of completion? _____
      _____
      _____

Completing the Circle of Love

2. God loves us and we love God in return. In a sense, the circle of God's love is completed when we love Him in return. However, John says that God's love is made complete when we love one another. What is his point (1 John 4:12)? _____
   _____

Love is the Motivator

3. What was necessary for all of the great actions listed by Paul in 1 Corinthians 13:1-3 to be profitable? _____
   _____
   _____

A. Besides love, what other possible motives could there be for doing these good works? _____

_____

4. **Discussion:** Read through Paul's definition of love in 1 Cor. 13:4-7. How does this definition help us understand love as the motivator in all of the "one another" qualities we have studied? Being "like-minded with one another" in mutually submitting to the message of the cross, "receiving one another" in areas of liberty, "bearing with one another", "bearing one another's burdens", "admonishing one another", "encouraging one another", "forgiving one another", "submitting and serving one another".

_____

_____

_____

_____

5. Thought question: Read through 1 Cor. 13:4-7 again substituting your name for the word "love". Does your name fit well? Which aspect do you need to work on most? _____

_____

_____

www.ingramcontent.com/pod-product-compliance
Lightning Source LLC
Chambersburg PA
CBHW070634050426
42450CB00011B/3195